Introc

Welcome to your EMl
This guide is here to support you in processing
challenging experiences through gentle,
structured exercises.

What You'll Find in This Workbook

This workbook is divided into five sections,
each with its own exercises to help you on your
healing journey.

You'll find prompts for grounding,
self-reflection, and understanding your
emotions, along with practical tips and strategies
to cope with trauma

Each section includes prompts and guidance
for how these can aid your journey, providing
tools for building self-compassion and
resilience.

At the end of the workbook, you'll find a
reflection questionnaire, allowing you to look
back on your progress, recognize areas of
growth, and set intentions for your ongoing
journey.

Take your time, go at your own pace, and
remember that each small step is a step forward.
Healing is a journey, and this workbook is here
to support you along the way.

How This Workbook Helps

This workbook provides EMDR-inspired exercises to support your healing journey.

Each section focuses on a key aspect of recovery:

Grounding Techniques
Learn methods to stay present and calm, helping you manage intense emotions and find stability.

Processing Emotions and Memories
Gentle prompts guide you to explore difficult memories in small, manageable ways, reducing their emotional weight.

Building Coping Skills
Practical tips and strategies give you effective tools for handling stress and challenging emotions.

Self-Compassion Practices
Exercises encourage self-kindness and help shift negative self-talk, allowing you to approach yourself with more empathy.

Reflection and Growth
An end-of-workbook questionnaire helps you look back on your progress, recognize your growth, and set intentions for moving forward.

How to Use This Workbook

1. Set aside time each day or week to focus on a prompt or a section. Consistency will help you make progress.

2. Read each prompt carefully and take time to reflect on your responses. Don't rush—give yourself space to think deeply.

3. Write honestly about your thoughts and feelings. The more open you are, the more helpful the process will be.

4. Use the tips and strategies provided in the workbook to support your answers and actions.

5. Review your progress regularly by looking back at previous entries. This will help you see how your thinking has changed over time.

6. Complete the end-of-workbook reflection to summarize your journey and recognize the growth you've made.

Section 1: Building a Foundation of Safety and Stability

This section focuses on establishing a sense of safety and calm.

Trauma can leave you feeling vulnerable, but with grounding exercises and soothing practices, you'll be able to create an emotional anchor.

These prompts provide techniques for feeling secure and prepared to manage any overwhelming moments.

Safe Place Visualization

Describe a place where you feel completely safe. What does it look, sound, and feel like?

Picture this place whenever stress or discomfort arises.

How it helps

Imagining a safe place activates calming pathways in your brain, helping you find relief from anxiety and stress.

Creating a Supportive Inner Voice

Write down a comforting phrase or statement you can say to yourself when feeling stressed or unsafe.

Think of it as a form of self-compassion and care.

How it helps

A supportive inner voice can replace self-criticism and offers comfort during difficult moments.

Physical Soothing Exercise

List three actions (like hugging yourself, deep breathing, or holding a soothing object) that bring you comfort.

When might these actions help you the most?

How it helps

Simple physical techniques help you connect with the present, releasing tension and soothing nerves.

Anchor Memory

Describe a memory where you felt loved, strong, or safe. Include sensory details.

Practice recalling this memory during stressful times.

How it helps

Remembering positive experiences can help shift your focus, providing emotional stability when you need it.

Strength Inventory

Identify three strengths that have supported you in challenging times.

How might they help you on this path?

How it helps

Acknowledging your strengths reminds you of your inner resources and increases confidence in handling emotions.

Personal Mantra

Create a simple phrase that reminds you of your courage and capacity for healing.

Repeat it to yourself during difficult moments.

How it helps

A mantra can center your mind, giving you strength to face distressing memories or feelings.

Visualization of Boundaries

Imagine a protective boundary around yourself that keeps out unwanted emotions or memories.

Describe what it feels like.

How it helps

Visualizing boundaries offers a sense of control over your mental space, making it easier to manage intrusive thoughts.

Section 2: Processing Emotions

This section helps you safely explore the emotions linked to trauma.

Processing emotions can reduce their intensity, making them easier to understand and manage.

These prompts provide simple ways to examine and work through feelings at a steady pace.

Naming Emotions

List the emotions you often
feel related to your trauma.

How strong are these
feelings?

How it helps

Identifying and naming
emotions allows you to work
through them without feeling
completely overwhelmed.

Emotional Timeline

Create a timeline of events that brought up strong emotions.

Describe each feeling in detail.

How it helps

Tracing emotional patterns can help you understand why certain emotions show up and when.

Body Scan Exercise

Notice each part of your body, from head to toe, and jot down any tension or sensations you feel.

How it helps

Trauma can reside in the body. Recognizing tension points helps you release stored stress and discomfort.

Emotion-to-Action Plan

For each emotion, write a
helpful action you can take
(e.g., taking a walk, journaling).

When could these actions
support you?

How it helps

Planning responses to
specific emotions gives you
practical tools, allowing you to
handle stress more effectively.

Expressive Writing

Spend five minutes writing about a recent emotional experience without editing yourself.

How it helps

This exercise helps you release thoughts and emotions, bringing a sense of relief and mental clarity.

Emotion Scaling

Choose an emotion you felt today, and rate its intensity from 1 to 10.

Reflect on what increased or decreased this intensity.

How it helps

Tracking intensity lets you see progress over time and helps you understand how certain situations affect your emotions.

Reframe Negative Thoughts

Identify a negative thought related to your trauma, then reframe it in a more positive or neutral light.

How it helps

Shifting your perspective helps reduce negative self-talk, encouraging a healthier outlook on yourself.

Section 3: Reprocessing Traumatic Memories

This section carefully introduces steps to revisit and reprocess traumatic memories.

Using EMDR-inspired techniques, you'll learn how to safely approach these experiences, allowing your brain to reframe them in a way that reduces their emotional intensity.

Memory Exploration

Choose a mild memory
associated with your trauma.

Write down what you
remember without judgment.

How it helps

Facing memories in a gradual
way allows you to process
them safely, which can reduce
their power over time.

Shifting Perspective

Write about the memory
from an outside,
compassionate perspective, as
if you were a kind friend.

How it helps

Observing the event from
another perspective promotes
self-compassion and can help
reduce shame or guilt.

Positive Ending Visualization

Imagine the traumatic memory ending differently, in a way that feels safe or positive.

Describe the new ending.

How it helps

Re-imagining events helps "reprogram" the memory, making it feel less threatening.

Distress Level Check

Rate your distress about this
memory from 1 to 10.

Reflect on what might help
lower this number.

How it helps

Tracking distress allows you
to monitor progress and adjust
your coping strategies as
needed.

Supportive Affirmations

Write three affirmations reminding you of your resilience.

How it helps

Positive affirmations can strengthen your belief in your ability to cope, boosting confidence and calm.

Gentle Tapping Exercise

Try gently tapping each side of your body while thinking about the memory.

Write about how it feels.

How it helps

Bilateral tapping has been shown to calm the nervous system, helping you feel less anxious as you process the memory.

Post-Reflection

Reflect on how you feel after working on this memory.

What insights have you gained?

How it helps

Reflection offers closure and helps you integrate new insights, giving you a sense of progress.

Section 4: Strengthening Self-Compassion and Self-Acceptance

This section centers on self-compassion, an essential part of the healing journey.

Trauma often leaves us with self-blame or feelings of unworthiness.

Through these prompts, you'll practice being kinder to yourself, recognizing your intrinsic worth, and embracing all parts of who you are.

Self-Kindness Letter

Write a letter to yourself as
if you were speaking to a close
friend who has gone through
similar experiences.

Offer encouragement and
compassion.

How it helps

Practicing kindness toward
yourself builds
self-compassion, helping
reduce self-criticism and
blame.

Mirror Exercise

Stand in front of a mirror, look into your eyes, and say, "I am worthy of love and care."

Write about the experience.

How it helps

This exercise reinforces self-acceptance, making it easier to view yourself with empathy and respect.

Embrace Your Strengths

List five qualities or strengths that you appreciate about yourself.

Think about how these have supported you through difficult times.

How it helps

Recognizing your strengths can bolster self-worth, reminding you that you have valuable traits to lean on.

Releasing Self-Blame

Write about any feelings of self-blame or guilt you may be holding.

Then, gently challenge those thoughts, reminding yourself of the truth.

How it helps

Letting go of self-blame can provide emotional relief and allows space for healing without added guilt.

Forgiving Yourself

Think of one thing you wish to forgive yourself for.

Write down a forgiveness statement, like "I forgive myself for..."

How it helps

Self-forgiveness is a powerful way to release negative emotions, making it easier to move forward with compassion.

Accepting Your Journey

Reflect on how far you've come since you started healing.

Write down ways you've grown and positive changes you've noticed.

How it helps

Acknowledging your growth helps you see healing as a journey, building patience and pride in your progress.

Daily Affirmation

Create a simple affirmation that you can say each morning, like "I am enough" or "I am worthy of happiness."

How it helps

Positive affirmations reinforce self-acceptance, encouraging a mindset that promotes healing and well-being.

Section 5: Moving Forward with Purpose and Hope

This section looks ahead, helping you envision a life beyond trauma.

These prompts guide you to set intentions, imagine positive possibilities, and identify support systems that can sustain you.

This section encourages a sense of hope, allowing you to focus on the future you want to create.

Future Vision

Describe your ideal future where trauma no longer has control over your life.

What does this look like?
How do you feel?

How it helps

Imagining a positive future can inspire hope, motivating you to take steps toward that vision.

Setting Intentions

Write down one or two intentions for your healing journey.

What changes do you want to see?

How it helps

Intentions provide a sense of direction, helping you stay focused on creating the life you want.

Support Circle

Identify people or resources that provide support and encouragement.

How can they help you stay on track?

How it helps

Knowing who or what supports you reinforces a sense of community, reminding you that you're not alone.

Daily Grounding Practice

Choose a small daily practice, like deep breathing or a gratitude journal, to help you stay centered.

How it helps

A grounding practice can provide stability, allowing you to handle life's challenges with greater calm.

Celebrating Small Wins

Reflect on three small wins you've experienced in your healing journey.

How do these accomplishments make you feel?

How it helps

Celebrating small victories acknowledges progress, boosting confidence and encouraging further growth.

Setting Healthy Boundaries

List areas in your life where you need boundaries to protect your well-being.

Write down ways to uphold these boundaries.

How it helps

Setting boundaries reinforces self-respect and ensures that your needs and limits are honored.

Gratitude Reflection

Write down three things
you're grateful for today.

How do they bring comfort
and positivity into your life?

How it helps

Practicing gratitude shifts
your focus toward what brings
joy, building a foundation for a
hopeful outlook.

Tips and Strategies

As you work through this workbook, having helpful tips and strategies can make your healing journey easier.

These simple suggestions are here to support you.

By using these strategies, you can create a positive environment for yourself that encourages healing and growth.

Think of each tip as a step toward feeling better and becoming stronger.

1. Establish a Safe Space for Self-Reflection

How to Do It

Designate a calm, comforting space where you feel at ease.

This could be a room with soothing colors, soft lighting, or objects that give you comfort (e.g., blankets, music, meaningful photos).

Set aside dedicated time each day or week to reflect in this space, letting yourself process thoughts and feelings without distractions.

Why It Helps

A safe space encourages relaxation and grounding, helping you to open up emotionally while feeling secure.

2. Practice Deep Breathing for Emotional Regulation

How to Do It

Find a quiet place, sit comfortably, and place one hand on your chest and the other on your abdomen.

Breathe in slowly through your nose, letting your abdomen expand, and then exhale slowly through your mouth.

Aim to repeat for a few minutes, focusing on the breath.

Why It Helps

Deep breathing activates the body's relaxation response, which can reduce stress and help you stay calm when processing difficult emotions.

3. Use a Daily Journaling Routine to Track Progress

How to Do It

Set a consistent time each day for journaling, even if only for five minutes.

Write about any changes, thoughts, or emotional shifts you notice.

Reflect on both the challenges and moments of relief in your journey.

Why It Helps

Tracking progress can make improvements visible, providing encouragement and a sense of accomplishment as you look back on how far you've come.

4. Practice Grounding Techniques to Manage Flashbacks

How to Do It

When feeling overwhelmed, try grounding by focusing on the present moment.

Use the "5-4-3-2-1" method: identify five things you can see, four you can touch, three you can hear, two you can smell, and one you can taste.

Take it slow, giving each step your full attention.

Why It Helps

Grounding keeps you connected to the present, helping to reduce the intensity of flashbacks or intrusive memories by engaging the senses.

5. Establish Boundaries to Protect Your Mental Health

How to Do It

Identify areas in your life where you need boundaries, like limiting time with people who may be unsupportive.

Practice stating your boundaries calmly and respectfully, such as saying, "I need some time alone right now" or "I'll need to think about that before deciding."

Why It Helps

Boundaries create a protective space for healing, allowing you to focus on your well-being without external pressure or stress.

6. Engage in Gentle Physical Activity

How to Do It

Try activities like walking, stretching, or yoga, moving at a pace that feels comfortable for you.

Aim for even 10-15 minutes daily, focusing on how your body feels during the movement rather than pushing yourself too hard.

Why It Helps

Gentle activity releases tension and stress, helping to process and release emotions that might be "stored" in the body from traumatic experiences.

7. Identify and Challenge Negative Self-Talk

How to Do It

Notice when you have self-critical thoughts and gently challenge them.

Ask yourself, "Is this thought true? Is there another way to look at this situation?"

Replace negative thoughts with more balanced, supportive ones.

Why It Helps

Challenging negative self-talk can reduce feelings of shame or guilt, fostering a more supportive internal dialogue that aids in the healing process.

8. Engage in Visualization for a Hopeful Future

How to Do It

Close your eyes and visualize a future where trauma no longer holds you back. Picture yourself feeling happy, free, and engaged in meaningful activities.

Take note of how this vision feels, and repeat this exercise regularly to build hope.

Why It Helps

Visualization promotes optimism and motivation by helping you see a version of yourself that has grown through challenges.

9. Celebrate Wins to Reinforce Progress

How to Do It

Each week, reflect on a few small accomplishments or moments of strength, like speaking kindly to yourself or sticking to a healthy routine.

Note these down in a journal or even share them with a trusted friend.

Why It Helps

Acknowledging progress, no matter how small, reinforces a positive view of your healing journey and can help sustain your motivation.

End-of-Workbook Reflection Questionnaire

These reflection questions encourage you to review and celebrate your progress.

They help reinforce what you've learned and identify the techniques that work best for you.

By reflecting on your journey, you gain a sense of accomplishment and clarity for moving forward confidently.

What is one key insight or lesson you've learned about yourself while working through this workbook?

(Helps you acknowledge self-discovery and growth, highlighting a meaningful takeaway from your journey.)

How have your feelings toward your trauma changed since you began this workbook?

(Encourages you to assess emotional shifts, helping you recognize progress in your relationship with past experiences.)

What coping strategies from the workbook have you found most helpful, and why?

(Focuses on practical tools, helping you identify which strategies resonate and can be used in the future.)

What is something you feel proud of accomplishing as you worked through these exercises?

(Offers an opportunity to celebrate your efforts and reinforce positive self-acknowledgment.)

Are there any areas where you
feel you need more support or
growth? How can you seek that
support moving forward?

(Encourages self-awareness
and planning, helping you
identify any areas that may
benefit from continued focus
or external help.)

What are your hopes or intentions for the next phase of your healing journey?

(Helps you envision a positive path forward, setting intentions for ongoing healing and personal growth.)

Closing Thoughts

Congratulations on reaching the end of this
EMDR Trauma Workbook!

Taking the time to explore these exercises is a
meaningful step toward healing, and every
moment you invested in reflection, grounding,
and growth is an accomplishment.

Remember, healing is a journey, and each
insight or skill you've developed here will
continue to support you in your everyday life.

You now have tools for processing difficult
memories, grounding yourself, and approaching
your emotions with self-compassion.

Use them whenever you need, and revisit the
exercises as often as feels right.

As you move forward, take pride in your
resilience and courage.

This workbook is just one chapter in your
journey, and with each step, you are creating
space for strength, peace, and growth.

Zooga Press

Made in the USA
Las Vegas, NV
11 December 2024

13878981R00066